ANCHORAGE

ANCHORAGE

Eleanor Zuercher

Copyright © 2024 Eleanor Zuercher

The moral right of the author has been asserted.

The scripture quotations contained herein are from the New Revised Standard Version Bible: Anglicised Edition, copyright © 1989, 1995 the Division of Christian Education of the National Council of the Churches of Christ in the United States of America, and are used by permission. All rights reserved.

Apart from any fair dealing for the purposes of research or private study, or criticism or review, as permitted under the Copyright, Designs and Patents Act 1988, this publication may only be reproduced, stored or transmitted, in any form or by any means, with the prior permission in writing of the publishers, or in the case of reprographic reproduction in accordance with the terms of licences issued by the Copyright Licensing Agency. Enquiries concerning reproduction outside those terms should be sent to the publishers.

This is a work of fiction. Names, characters, businesses, places, events and incidents are either the products of the author's imagination or used in a fictitious manner. Any resemblance to actual persons, living or dead, or actual events is purely coincidental.

Troubador Publishing Ltd
Unit E2 Airfield Business Park,
Harrison Road, Market Harborough,
Leicestershire LE16 7UL
Tel: 0116 279 2299
Email: books@troubador.co.uk
Web: www.troubador.co.uk

ISBN 978 1 805145 36 3

British Library Cataloguing in Publication Data.
A catalogue record for this book is available from the British Library.

Printed and bound in the UK by TJ Books Limited, Padstow, Cornwall
Typeset in 11pt Adobe Garamond Pro by Troubador Publishing Ltd, Leicester, UK

This book is dedicated to its readers, with my appreciative thanks.

We have this hope, a sure and stedfast anchor of the soul, a hope that enters the inner shrine behind the curtain
(Hebrews, 6:19)

CONTENTS

SIGHT

The Lies of a Mirror	3
Chlorine Blue	4
Fiat Nox	5
Octagon on the Isle of Ely	6
Of an Overhanging Tree	7
The Mill Stream at Towcester	8
"The eye is the lamp of the body…"	9
"But they kept asking him, 'Then how were your eyes opened?'"	13

SOLITUDE

Silence	17
Anchorage	24
Freedom	29
I Am Not	33
I Lift Up My Eyes	35
Saturday People *Memento Mori*	36
Shut the Door	37

SKIRMISH

Afraid	41
The Lessons of a Spider	42
De Profundis	45
Emmanuel	46
If I'd Been There	47
Nicodemus's Song	49
Prodigal	50
Simon of Cyrene	56
The Veil was Torn in Two	57
Christmas Lost	58
Lockdown Christmas	59
Forest Stations in Lincoln Cathedral	60
As Pants the Hart	61

SOLACE

At the Ebb	65
Christmas Present	66
Friendship	67
In Remembrance	68
The Lord is an Enigma	69
The Word of the Lord Is	70
Which Passes All Understanding	71
Worcester Cathedral Triptych	73
Jellyfish	75
Cherry Tree in Winter	76
Acknowledgements	78

Sight

The Lies of a Mirror

Though I know it to be a thin pane
Of silvered glass, it contains,
Switched left to right, the room behind me.
It is a lie, without depth.

It shows an almost accurate reflection
Of an unanimated face
Which I know truly from inside –
Almost convincing. But not quite.

Chlorine Blue

Chlorine-blue water, lit by sunshine,
Generates its own luminosity,
Languidly waving ripples across the roof

To crawl lazily, like a slow, cool fire,
Smoothing with its milky turquoise tongue
To warm the tiles and soothe pine beams.

In imitation, the caster of the spell
Quietly shivers in the pool, completing
The illusion of watery enclosure.

Fiat Nox

Our craving for light and certainty is such
That homes and streets and cities are submerged
In such a flood of light, that darkness is hard
To find, and urban glow afflicts the night
For miles around, with power enough to dim
Even the brightest stars and suns. And yet
However bright the lights, however fierce
The summer sun, we fumble in dark unknowing.
Our condition is to be benighted, blind.
In devouring knowledge, absolutes,
We forget that, although from a vantage point
On a good day we can see for miles,
In darkness, we can see for light years,
Perhaps to that moment of *fiat lux*.

Octagon on the Isle of Ely

The way of life meanders, all at sea,
Drawn to the sunlit octagon, where
It seems possible to reach the eighth day
Without cycling round the mundane seven;
And where the eighth colour of the spectrum
Is in amongst the flooding light thundering
Through the glass above, both raining down
And drawing up; both drowning and bathing.

Of an Overhanging Tree

On the brightest summer's day,
The light reflected off a stream
And thickly rippling up the bark
Of an overhanging tree
Can seem like silent,
Luminous, heavy rainfall
Streaming over a rooflight.

But in the sombre winter,
Sullen yellow light
Gleaming through
The pounding torrent battering
My rooflight is a world away
From light reflected off a stream
And thickly rippling up the bark

Of an Overhanging Tree.

The Mill Stream at Towcester

Even in sunset moments of glassy reflection,
Undercurrents steer the languid water
With undeniable, unopposable purpose.

One drop of water can bend and shake trees
Or ancient bridges while ducks trailing wakes
Tug scudding clouds counter to the wind.

Cats' paws shiver branches, birds and faces
Into an insect world of compound vision,
A kaleidoscope of churning, glowing fragments.

Fine rain hisses and dances, perpetually shifting
In the interstices of heavy droplets,
Or the flick of fish broadcasting concentric
Rings, spooling from each centre, crossing
And recrossing in strobing, spirographic shimmer.

"THE EYE IS THE LAMP OF THE BODY..."
(Matthew 6:22)

I Ye That Have Eyes To See

I would not glare balefully with an evil eye;
I would not gaze uncritically with a sheep's eye;
I would not scan broadly with an elephant's eye;
I would not inspect minutely with a worm's eye;
I would not scrutinise piercingly with an eagle's eye;
I would not look blindly with a peacock's eye:
I would view imaginatively with the mind's eye;
I would discern compassionately with the heart's eye;
I would contemplate faithfully with the soul's eye;
I would see clearly with the spirit's eye.

II A Healthy Eye

Eyes are easily deceived by sleight
Of hand, smoke and mirrors, dust blown, wool pulled.
Light can be bent, refracted, diffused, filtered,
And even a healthy eye absorbing the wonder
Displayed in an infinite universe,
Disbelieves magnificence. To see rightly,
Or truly, or clearly, may be impossible.

God's light cannot be so manipulated.
Our truth is not his truth; our light is not
His light. His light may outrun or exceed
Physics and requires a better organ
Than a human eye to see it and see by it.
Eyes are not to be entrusted, without
The added perspective of heart, mind and soul.

III Interface

An evil eye looking for fault will find it
And, infected with what it finds, will bathe
All that within in dark, distorted light
Refracted through an ailing, twisted lens;
The inner darkness, now intensified,
Reflects fault back, balefully magnified,
Into the world without.

A kindly eye
Gazes compassionately and mercifully
On sin but always seeks for something better.
This, once found, freshens and restores
The world within, and thence illuminates
The beam of the returning gaze.

The eye is the interface where within
Meets without. Worlds cross. Without
Informs within; within interprets without.

IV "The Eye Is the Lamp of the Body…" *(Matthew 6:22)*

Be careful what you look for. Evil and error
Are not hard to find, encompassing,
In black and white and fizzing electrical colour.
But the seeking after hatred, fear, distrust
Only and inevitably ensures its finding.

It is harder to find the micro-seeds of love
Or droplets of joy in dust, in pain, in blood –
This requires patiently sifting detritus,
And an eager eye to spot goodness glinting,
Nestling quietly, untainted, alongside decay.

Seek and ye shall find. But be careful
What you look for.

V Consequences

In Adam's disobedience, his eyes
Opened to myriad possibilities,
And must have flit around the fresh new garden,
Bewildered at such complex, baffling potential.
But a broader vision resulted in focus lost
At the final, fatally echoing clang of the gate.

But when, in his obedience, Christ
Closed his eyes in that crimson pain,
And later lay so still, eyes bandaged shut,

In the deep, chill darkness, the gate swung open
And light dawned again in the reciprocal
Chiming of glorious re-creation.

VI Windows of the Soul

Perhaps the eye cannot hide
The thoughts of the heart, but that truth
Is only legible to an unclouded eye
And clearest heart.

Otherwise another's eye will only
Reflect my own, and all I then
Will see therein is my own trust,
Or distrust;

My own worthiness or unworthiness;
A shadow of my love, or fear.
Eyes are not the windows of the soul
But its mirrors.

"But they kept asking him, 'Then how were your eyes opened?'"

(John 9:10)

I Interview with the Man Lately Blind

    He opened my eyes.

But who performed this act?
And how did he do it? And why?
But what was in it for him?
And whereabouts did this happen?

    He opened my eyes.

What time and date was this?
The experience in three words?
But why do you think he chose you?
Anything to say to him?

    He opened my eyes.

What kind of trick did he use?
Did money change hands?
Where do you think he is now?
Can we get tickets?

      He opened my eyes.

No one asks:

      Can he open my eyes too?

II And Now I See

I cannot tell how sight crawled out of mud,
How light began to shine into eyes sealed
And caked in earth, but a barely perceptible glimmer
Began rising, glowing, heating and pulsing into the full,
Effulgent splendour of unaccustomed light.

It took a while to assimilate the fact
Of sight, to feast on unimagined glories,
To bathe in colour and shade and shape and depth,
In expressions of faces beloved, and be replete;
Before the detail of the truth I'd missed

Spilled across my retinas, misunderstandings,
Misconceptions, plain mistakes displayed
In glorious certainty and full perspective.
The precious gift of vision is not without
Cost, but I would not be blind again.

Solitude

Silence

"...we look not at what can be seen but at what cannot be seen..."

(2 Corinthians 4:18)

We also listen not for what can be heard but what cannot be heard.

I Perception

The hearing of silence is impossible.
There is no place sufficiently inert
To overturn my simple, unfledged senses,
For I can perceive only light;
I can hear only sound;
I can touch only matter;
I can smell only scent.
How can I know what is silence?
How can I know what is darkness?

In a state of life,
How can I know what is death?

II Unheard Voices

A few voices can be heard easily
And clearly, but the strange, unnatural silence
Of the dispossessed and powerless,
Is like a film muted, without colour,
And refracted through thick, distorting glass.

Watching from privilege, gazing with longing
Either backwards or forwards to the Eden
We had once and yearn to reattain.
There is another screen beyond our reach
Through which we persist in praying hearing.

What sounds penetrate there?

III Silent Secrecy

Wrapped in silence I become invisible
And can slip easily through a hustling crowd
Unremarked, alone and insulated.

Clutching to myself opinion, thought
And feeling in unrevealing isolation;
Silence is the ultimate disguise.

Though impenetrable in crowds, silence,
When endured with just one other, is more
Catastrophically revealing than speech.

IV Silencing

The violence of silence is threat and fear;
It smothers, muzzles and conceals.
A sign of vanquishment –
The repressed are silent

But watching.

V No Stillness in Silence

Silence isn't always still.
That bowel-wrenching, whining (almost) silence,
Which squeezes the lungs and sings soundlessly
In the ears, is full of grinding menace.

Silence is always the last one standing.
It cannot be overcome.
It always has the last un-word.
So it must be enjoined, and sought.

Welcome and embrace it as a brother,
Before you meet it hereafter as a foe.

VI Filling a Silence

Nature does not abhor a vacuum – mostly
Nature is vacuum – but we dislike
A void.

We combat it by throwing sound, any
Sound, into the silent, anechoic, sucking
Well.

The sound is drowned instantly, as though
It had never been, without hint
Or sigh.

Any, all and every sound is swathed
In the final universal void –
In vacuum,

Unheard, unhearable and far beyond
Apprehension, in the silent yawning vastness
Of space.

VII Crushing Silence

Silence is adamantine, its crushing mass
Presses smothering on jittery ears,
As it stalks with darkness, hand in hand.

They are vanquishers. They populate
The shadows of unease and ill-deeds;
They are feared and comprehended well.

Yet these primal monsters are illusive,
Easily disquieted, banished
By a candle flame, a word. For now.

VIII A Positive Choice

Silence is more than the absence of sound.
It is a blessed liberation
From its persistent tyranny.
A positive, discerning choice.
Crystal, undisturbed water;
Air in suspension; pure stillness.
Not an absence, but a presence,
Timorous, shrinking, yet glorious.
So fine, so delicate, as to be
Beyond perceiving. So rare. So perfect.

IX Silent Spaces

Silence is weightlessness, unencumbered
In a bright white light-filled room,
Where the anima can adjust, expand,
And tendrils of thought float unimpeded.
The mind inhales and flexes its percipience,
Finds its own connections in itself
And beyond. Here is my breathing space,
My mind's cure and heart's inspiration –
Silence is the oxygen of the soul.

X A Rare Commodity

Silence, though a coin of great rarity,
Encroaches on all things. Though fragmented,
It increasingly encompasses my soul,
Gathering mass, momentum, significance.

Silence between words,
Anticipating the meaning of the next;

Silence between stanzas,
Accumulating flows of wondering;

Silence at the end of a play,
Replete with satisfying resolution;

Silence preceding speech,
Brimming with uncertain potential.

Like the silence between worlds,

The interstitial silence between cells,

Between atoms.

Between one breath.
                        And the next.

And what of my final silence…?

XI Silence of the Grave

What we think is silence is not.

It is the sigh of breeze,
                        The scuttle of beetle,
An electric reverberation,
                        The pulsing of blood.

Even the silence of the grave

Is the slow seeping of water
                              Through grains of soil,
The gathering of an earthworm.
                              And heave of continents.

On this digesting, living planet,

There is no silence.

XII Listening to Silence

God speaks with the profoundest silence,
Addressing a mind which hears only
Sound, a soul untuned to stillness,
A heart whose pulsing banishes quiet.

My doubtful faith is a vacillating shimmer;
My fearful hope is shivering fragments;
My feeble love uncomprehending;
My unknowing prayer blind silence.

And yet I am encompassed. I am heard.

Anchorage

I What Holds Me Now?

When granite passes like water through my fingers,
And seasoned oak shudders and fragments,
When steel clasps and hasps dissolve in steam,
What holds me then?

When flesh bleeds and bleeds and will not stint,
When organs fail, fold and liquefy,
And soft skin frays and bone crumbles,
What holds me then?

When gravity rejects me, and my eyes
Are blind to light, when, in a liquid world,
Only I am adamantine stone,
Who will catch me now?

II Sealed in Cells

I make a life in death, and accept
My death in life. My freedom is enclosed
And bound, sealed by the fact of dust, blood,
Time and gravity. I squint with narrowed
Vision in hope of some perspective.
I am helpless to prevent encroachment,

That human overlap, with those I serve;
Those who serve me. I find myself in a cell
Constructed of cells, a decaying case to seal in
The soul. But can the soul learn lightness in the dark
Or freedom in bonds? What can it risk in safety?

But perhaps it can risk nothing without it.

Set me as a seal upon your heart.

III Anchorage

I am implanted in my now, rooted
In the topography of my here;
Made fast by age, gender and bleeding still;
Tangled in obligation and perception;
Pinioned by routine tending of body and soul;
Embedded in the physics of dust, water
And gravity; my isolation clawed at
By encroaching nature, my darkness pierced
By light, my loneliness bruised by love; enclosed
By, and in, what I know myself to be.

IV Loosing Chains

What tender precious bonds are those
Which set a seal upon my life.
So anchored by a granite love
For and of my dearest ones,

I cleave to the freshening whisper of rain,
And delight in the whirl of dancing of words,
I rejoice in that summoning back from the brink
By pitch-dark birdsong shadowing dawn.

These lightest of tethers secure me more surely
Than stone or steel, but will these habits
Of clay, when such soothing bonds are loosed,

Make me prefer the weary chains
Of pain and illness and irrelevance
To the risking of all in free flight?

V Gift of Silence

Words which once paraded across the pages
And lined up in my mind in proper order
Now fail. They are not adequate for expression.
Instead, I receive the gift of silence, not black
And white and solid like print, a definite meaning,
But sinuous to fill the silent spaces like honey,
And solidifying to support the absence
Of certainty; not angular but soft; not tart but sweet
To cushion the mind and senses.

VI Words

Words which touch or speak
By rote; which bind and free;
Which wound and heal; make solid,

Mould, flex and dissolve;
Which both beguile and repel,
Can skewer thought and action
Or slide by barely noticed;
Can lodge in the soul for ever
Or evaporate in an instant;
They spill uncontrolled
Or drop tightly constrained;
They seal and cut loose;
Of unimaginable
Power – and of none;
They are tools to enable thought
And a means of avoiding it.
A word cannot enclose
Meaning any more than a cell
Can enclose a flickering soul,
Infinitely varied
Yet widely understood.
Plain speech set in code
And paradox crystalised.

VII Living the Dream

I sought safety but found danger;
I desired certainty but discovered doubt;
I pleaded for shelter but was exposed;
I dreamt of flight but was shackled to earth;
I hoped for success but must own to weakness.
How strange then, that I should find
In weakness, the humility for learning;

In shackles, the meaning of freedom;
In exposure, the seed of faith;
From doubt, the necessity of trust;
And from danger, a rooted steadfastness.

Freedom

I Freedom Is…

Freedom is a glorious lacking –
Free from wheat, dairy, nuts,
Free from additives and E-numbers,
Free from fat and sugar and taste.

Freedom is abandoning control –
Free speech, free press, free-for-all,
Freestyle, free country, free love,
Freewheeling, free fall.

Freedom costs nothing –
Free to air, duty-free,
Kids go free, free and easy,
Free gift, buy one, get one free.

But true freedom is dense,
Not lacking; it demands control
Because it imposes responsibility,
And therefore it costs everything.

II Impossibility of Freedom

Freedom is an impossibility.
There is no freedom from demands of time,
Year by year, week by week, minute
By slippery minute; or my corporeal bonds,
A countdown, breath by breath, heartbeat by heartbeat –
Incarceration of a lively spirit,
Manacled to dust by gravity.
There is freedom from biology
Only in the prison of a grave,
And physics wields the slenderest lead
In the anechoic void of open space.

III Longing

I long for freedom.
I flee to feel grass, green beneath my feet,
The sky stretched blue and wide above my head,
But I am curtailed by boundaries –
Fences, rivers, thickets, walls, escarpments.

I long for freedom.
I set full sail on the broad and shifting ocean,
Scanning boundless, changeless grey horizon,
But am governed by the swell, current,
Wind, tide, the push and pull of the moon.

I long for freedom.
I try the hover and swoop of a kestrel's flight –

In free air there is neither tether nor stay –
But am hobbled by gravity, drag,
My own weight and ineffective wings.

But I long for freedom,
So I turn away, leaving what I know;
I break the nagging tug of gravity,
The inconvenience of air resistance.

In deep space,

        Alone,

                In soundless

                      Vast

                              Nothingness,

I no longer recall the weight of the burden
From which I longed to be free.

IV The Unwanted Gift

I recognise, with a shrinking heart,
The reappearance of the unvalued gift
Which tours the raffles and tombolas
And which I promptly rewrap (to disguise),
And return to circulation.

So, I seal my heart in another's keeping;
I squander my eagerness on a cause – any cause –
I submit my time to earning a living,
When I am already living, and expect
God (or fate) to dictate my choices.
So I no longer make my own
Mistakes, and unwanted free will is,
Most satisfactorily, silenced
And tightly trussed up for sacrifice.

V The Balance

There are no scales to measure and account
For emotion, power or faith. There is
No balance to measure payment of feeling or trust.

How could the execution of God do other
Than disturb the universal balance?
How could this be construed as fair payment
For the liabilities of human sin?

God's love is also unaccountable.

And only this gravity-defying
Gift could lighten the scale sufficiently
To balance our account. Only love
Makes equilibrium possible. Only
In equilibrium can there be freedom.

I Am Not

I am neither extraordinary
Nor ordinary;
I am neither knowledgeable
Nor ignorant;
I am neither fully alive
Nor dead;
I am neither good
Nor bad;
I am neither leader
Nor follower.

I am only
Here.
Only now.

To forge an identity
From position, or skill,
I describe myself
As nurturer, friend.
And think of myself
As a chip of stone,
Or a mote of dust.

But under the infinite arch of sky
And the fathomless reach of stars,

Immersed in perfect blue
At the shadowed foot of the cross,

    Truly I am not.

I Lift Up My Eyes
(Psalm 121)

I lift up my eyes to the hills. What cometh thence
Is uncertain. The Lord who made heaven and earth,
Who never slumbers, who keeps me in his hand,
Who makes the streams to flow and trees to grow,
Also makes earth to shift, mountains
To buckle, boulders to roll and thunder, crushing
Down his cliffs and hillsides. God's loving kindness,
His care, and the refuge under His wings are often
Unnoticed, out of sight and mind. He is good.
But He is not safe. Nor tame. Nor solely mine.

Saturday People
Memento Mori

Saturday people wait
Between Friday and Sunday,
Between birth and dying
And between dying and birth,
In the shadow of death,
In the chill of the tomb.

If I take a moment
To look about me,
I know I wait also.
Life's distractions
Only delay
This recollection.

But here I am,
Between birth and dying,
Between Friday and Sunday,
Waiting in the shadow
For light, waiting
In the tomb for life.

Shut the Door
(Matthew 6:6; John 20:29)

Just shut the door,
Close the mind's
Postern on distraction.
The heart's latch
Secures the best place
For secret words,
The soul's thoughts
Uniquely focused,
In quiet seclusion,
Behind the door.

Skirmish

Afraid

I am so very well acquainted with fear.
I know I am afraid. I am afraid
That all I am is Afraid. What if
I have no organ or atom not constructed
From fear? What if, when all is stripped away,
I am only a quivering, walking terror,
Clothing bones which only dream of strength
And shielded by reality-deflecting
Skin. Afraid to live and afraid
Not to live. Is there no remedy?
What am I to do if the only
Cure is to face the One from whom
I have most to fear, and ask for grace?
Will there at last be love? Blessing?

The Lessons of a Spider

I Web

    I am surely drawn into a vortex towards the place
    I most desire to avoid and the person I least
    Desire to be. The centre of my worst self
    Hunkers, with its aiders and abettors,
    Whose baleful influence I cannot shake
    At the hub of a malevolent web,
    Twitching a sullen, silken trap,
    Manipulative, watchful,
    Absorbing my opposite
    Impulses, weaving
    The fabric
    Of a terrible
    Alter
    Ego.

II Arachnophobia

The fear lives in the twitch of any one
Of its legs, its aura of suspended action,
Its unpredictable watchfulness
And gravity-defying ability
To weave mid-air castles out of nothing.
It magnetises my gaze which cannot leave it

Unwatched. It waits. I am fascinated,
Drawn towards its web to gaze upon
The monster reflected in its many eyes.

III Bound and Gagged

The spider spins threads like fishing twine
To hook its prey and draw it in. Similar
Creatures weave upright indignation
And starchy adherence to an uncertain code of fairness,
Into narrative with power to pull
A mind into bitterness and drag
A soul into sour disappointment.
But the trap won't close until the victim
Gives consent.
And I will not be stitched
Into its sticky toils.

IV Spider's Work

Finely twisting, twining, spinning,
Carefully stringing, threading, testing,
Patiently waiting, luring, glowering,
Expertly playing, tweaking, trapping,
Finally weaving, wrapping, feasting.

V Unheard Music

What wondrous sounds must a musician spider
Create, stretching and tuning her sighing threads,

Weaving new twist and pitch into her own geometry,
Spinning and stringing an inaudible harmony,
Wrapped in the humming of her own silky oscillation,
Whether ringing with dew, or sharpened by frost,
Tautened by the shrill heat of the sun,
Or booming with fresh prey or heavy raindrops.

DE PROFUNDIS
(Psalm 130)

Out of the depths, I cry to you, O Lord.
In the darkest deeps flicker and stir
Shadows of acts and sullen thoughts interred
    Where I dare not look.

Spectral fears scent the arid air.
Indistinctly shaped and veiled, their imprint
Leaves the pattern of the twisting net
    And desiccates the core.

Yet in the deep there is solidity;
A luminous and permeating stillness
    Echoes through ripening stone.

Here is sanctuary, certainty, resource;
These deeps form and secure my essence.

From the depths I watch for the morning, O Lord.

Emmanuel

What difference does it make for the light to shine in our midst?

We used to walk on short shadows
Which pooled blackly round our feet,
While brilliant light pounded blessing
On our heads in stark epiphany,
And the Word echoed through the hills.
Now the light shines among us,
So we trail, long confused,
Multiple shadows into illusory,
Inauspicious hiding places
Where the Word whispers fraternally.
The light obscured by prismatic flesh
Confounds perspective, disorientates.
Emmanuel. God with us.

If I'd Been There

If I'd been there
I'd have gaily waved palms with the rest,
Eager to see a celebrity.

If I'd been there
Issued with a shield, spear and armour,
I'd have followed orders.

If I'd been there
I'd have clutched my pennies in the temple
And been morally affronted.

If I'd been there
I'd have gossiped with my friends over tea –
"The innocent have nothing to fear."

If I'd been there
I'd have known that nice people have nice friends
And not looked past their faces.

If I'd been there
I would have made no difference – only one more
Guilty face in a guilty crowd.

Whether I was there
Or not, strangely, unaccountably,
I am forgiven.

Nicodemus's Song

In fear of being seen, or detected,
Edging round the shadows, slipping
Through society's interstices,
We come, in darkness, to the light.

From the comfortable velvet midnight,
Now dazzled and confused, shielding
Unseeing eyes from unaccustomed brightness,
We come to the light, in darkness.

Blind and unknowing, an unlearned spirit
Scrabbling for a light, a match,
Feeling for truth from truth, and light from light
We, in darkness, come to the light.

Out of ignorance and partial sight
Gleaned from a clouded mirror,
Blown like samaras by the unseen wind,
In darkness, we come to the light.

Prodigal

I Lost
When he had spent everything, a severe famine took place throughout that country and he began to be in need (Luke 15: 14)

I must have crossed a line some time ago,
Maybe in a dream, like the line between
Childhood and adult life, but now I find
Myself the other side of the border from home,
Regarding untraversable terrain.

Sometimes, when I suppose the wind to blow
From there, I taste the breeze, imagining
I can detect some familiar trace,
Although I have long forgotten what
Was familiar about a lost utopia.

That is where the dryness of my life
Can flower, where lacking is complemented,
Emptiness is filled, vapours made tangible,
And solitariness accompanied.
But in this waking life, a mirage, no more.

II Realisation

But when he came to himself he said "How many of my father's hired hands have bread enough and to spare, but here I am dying of hunger!" (Luke 15:17)

I awake at last. But I awake an exile.
The mirror shows my unfamiliar face
And unaccustomed clothing. My daily life
Is shaped by strangers' habits. I now dwell
In a foreign land, but I am not at home.
Cut off from home, family, purpose and exiled
From myself. My soul orients itself
On the place of its belonging, my feet
Following. I am surprised, into wholeness,
By meeting myself on the circuitous route,
For though God had been with me,
I had, for a while, departed from him.

III Home

I will get up and go to my father (Luke 15:18–19)

Home holds me – my resting and returning place.
I am drawn to it by love and longing,
My comfort and my hiding place,
My hope for forgiveness.

Home keeps me at a distance – by fear, shame
And guilt. It is my place of weakness
And the place of my nakedness,
My dread of discovery.

But love and yearning will persist in labouring
To outrun fear and conquer pain.
If it is truly home, a welcome
Will be waiting.

IV Waste

For all these years I have been working like a slave for you,
and I have never disobeyed your command (Luke 15:29)

So many things overlong desired
Are a waste of money, and activity,
With which we fill a life, turns out to be
A waste of time.

It is poor recompense for such generous
Abundance to trail a dusty, littered wasteland
Of resources squandered heedlessly
And left behind.

But a life unlived is as wasteful as a life
Overlived. A life of joyless prescription
Produces a dreadful harvest – a hardened heart
And narrow outlook.

Unexperienced passion, untried freedom,
Unasked questions and untested theories
Are all living opportunities,
Thoughtlessly wasted.

V Inheritance
So he divided his property between them (Luke 15:12)
Son, you are always with me, and all that is mine is yours.
(Luke 15:31)

So where is my inheritance?
Wasted? Risked on insubstantial folly?
Or kept secure and hoarded unused, unseen?

And what of my inheritors?
Has the treasure blown away in heated winds?
Or been reduced, in storage, to dry, sour dust?

VI Prodigal Father
And get the fatted calf and kill it, and let us eat and
celebrate; for this son of mine was dead and is alive again;
he was lost and is found (Luke 15:23–24)

What divine profligacy!
The tumbling exuberance of stars and galaxies;
The intricate workings of universal movement
And precarious balance of gravity;
The heating and cooling of our tectonic planet,
Its weather patterns and living geography;
The greenness of goodness and blue infinity;
The self-sustaining torrent of life which overruns
Ocean, sky and land; the breath of trees;
And the human spirit and soul capable
Both of wonders and atrocities,
Love and fear, strength and appalling weakness,

The free expression of your varied creatures,
But mostly I wonder at your appetite
To forgive folly and evil –
Even at such a fearful cost, you meet us,
And treat us with what prodigal love!

VII Reunion

for this son of mine was dead and is alive again; he was lost and is found (Luke 15:24)
But we had to celebrate and rejoice, because this brother of yours was dead and has come to life; he was lost and has been found (Luke 15:32)

There is unbearable tension
In the rupture of what belongs together,
    Parent and child; mankind in Eden;
    God with his people. Like a lock and a key.
Reunion becomes the rapt focus
And purpose of existence.

The pain of cleaving from – the cutting and the severing,
    The joy of cleaving to – in reuniting and repairing,
Despair of a primal power displaced,
    Hope in the snap of magnets rejoining,
Seeking to restore energy disrupted,
    Finding synergy restored.

VIII Risk

And I? What kind of prodigal am I?
Leaning towards luxury and pleasure
Or preferring security, without risk?
Does he call me home or send me out?

Am I beckoned to safety or dared to danger?
Should I yearn for forgiveness or licence?
Am I able to awake his image in me?
Have I the nerve to let go of the branch?

I want to be the sheep who never leaves
The safety of the fold but who is still,
Nevertheless, the subject of rejoicing.
But investing nothing gains nothing.

If I could but be prodigal in love,
Risk or certainty would each be welcome,
I believe.

Simon of Cyrene

We know only that he bore
A crossbeam on the final steps
Of a criminal's last bloodstained journey.

Only that single spotlit moment.

Did he allow its aftermath
To shape his life to come? Or know
That act would be remembered and

Only that single spotlit moment?

God, in unexpected guises,
Lights unexpecting people. If He
Alighted on me, though I had nothing,

I'd have that spotlit blessed moment.

The Veil Was Torn in Two

When the roiling darkness pierced the sun
And ploughed with searing force across the sky,
When fissures scourged the wounded earth, the fearful
Tearing of God from forsaken God
Left Moses's veil a fraying rag and the order
Of nature, time and space unravelling.
So now when Adam's ever-seeking God
Calls out, "Where are you?", I see enough, even
In this blazing darkness, to reply,
"Here I wait not just with stained and sticky
Fingers but now with blood on my hands,
Expecting the fruit of an equal and opposite
Reaction, here I wait. I wait for love."

Christmas Lost

You never seem further away than at Christmas,
When shivering darkness presses in
Ominously, when I most seek courage,
When sunrise seems most in doubt,

I am never near enough to reach for,
Or speak to or gaze on you.
I cannot come close in crowded spaces;
I cannot discern your likeness in glitter
Or flashing lights;
                              I find no warmth
In overheated, airless rooms;
No nourishment in over-rich food;
No sense of achievement in the hectic
Ticking of lists; no sense of giving
In my dwindling bank account.

But perhaps, by now, I should know better
Than to seek the cold and threadbare
Refugee family in these places.

I should do better to look squarely
On the chilling darkness and seek you
Instead within my truthful fear.

Lockdown Christmas

Then, uneasy, the watchful authorities pace
The streets, and fear stirs at every threshold.
Shops are shut; there's no room to meet or to stay,
But an uncertain light flickers in the doorway.

A small, a secret thing.

No shout of celebration, but inaudible angels
Sing to the few who can hear, as animals settle,
Muffled into the straw of a shed perfumed
By the steaming breath and the dung of the cattle.

A silent, a secret thing.

A fragile couple, far from friends, lacking
The comfort of family at the intimate scene of a birth,
Roughly cushioned in hay, with strangers, shepherds,
Socially distant, to watch at the advent of hope.

A raw, a secret thing.

Forest Stations in Lincoln Cathedral

Christ follows the crushing ashen grain
As rough bark funnels the path
To the ebony guards who always wait
At the only possible destination.

The sharp-edged shadow of the cross
Gouges a wound through what I know
To be true. A dark fissure in reality –
To let the darkness out. Or in.

Midnight pools within the heartwood
Which shrouds it like a chrysalis,
Until the brightness is ready to flood
All creation without stint.

As Pants the Hart
(Psalm 42)

As a tree longs, unknowing, for sunshine,
A bird for flight, or a river for the valley,
As one who shivers, longs for warmth,
So longs my soul for thee, O God.

My daily diet has been busyness
By day; fear and doubt by night,
In a world where no one remembers
To speak of God (an irrelevance) at all.

There is no throng to sing, no multitude
To keep festival, but a few hold fellowship
Fast through the winter, waiting for spring,
For warmth, as the trees wait for sunshine.

Solace

At the Ebb

What joy there is in buoyancy on the waves,
What exhilaration in borrowing energy
From the flow which races to land, burdened
With the spectrum of light, a suspension of sand,
And churning life, to fling upon the shore.
But only when the buffeting generosity
Has subsided are its treasures revealed.
Then the ebb tide displays a newly minted
Shoreline. In the perfection of untouched sand,
Shine sparkling quartz chips, mussel shells
Glowing Prussian blue and trails of emerald
Seaweed lacing perfectly glazed pools.
Epiphany is in the soul's ebb:
The flood's promise completed in abatement.

Christmas Present

The first, best, Christmas present
        Was simply presence.
That moment of birth contained
        Also death,
And anticipated something
        More than death.

That present was not subject to time.
        Instead of becoming
Past, then forgotten, discarded and lost,
        It fell transcendent,
Into all sequential time,
        Like a drop

Of iridescent dye in water.
        That focused presence
Still irradiates our present.
        So the last best
Gift we can present is simply
        To be.

        Now.

Friendship

At the overlap, the intersection
Where lives, and sometimes hearts, minds or souls
Cross, there friendship germinates.
From a shadow of shared interest in dog walking
Or coffee drinking, or model train construction,
The overlap might grow, or might not.
It relies on mutual exposure, mutual risk.
I open part of my soul to share with you,
And you allow me to share in a portion of yours.

In Remembrance

We recast worthless tokens, fragments
Treasured past use or beauty to reshape
Memory of the lost and make anew
Those left behind, still remembering.

Spotted images reintegrate
Their jerking monochrome world with our own,
In a bugle's weeping, at the going down of the sun,
And the blood-red flutter of a November flower.

The weekly remembrance, sharing bread and wine,
Reincorporates each of us as organs
Of the body. Dry bones live once more,
Repurposed. In remembrance we are re-membered.

The Lord Is An Enigma
(Psalm 23)

The Lord is an enigma
Which I cannot understand.
He makes me to walk into uncertainty;
He leads me by deep waters
And under broad skies.
He speaks to my soul.
Yea, as I walk through shadow,
Though I fear evil,
You are with me
And maintain me.
You have named me,
Notwithstanding my failings,
And will welcome me
To dwell encompassed
In your breathing for ever.

The Word Of The Lord Is
(Psalm 19)

The word of the Lord is the pot of gold:
    More desirable than youth or beauty;
The word of the Lord is as easy as space travel:
    As difficult as breathing;
The word of the Lord challenges and provokes:
    And soothes and heals;
The word of the Lord is immoveable as ocean:
    And as fluid;
The word of the Lord is silent thunder:
    And still lightning;
The word of the Lord is a fertile desert
    Under a starlit sky;
As full of promise as birdsong in the rain
    On New Year's Day;
The word of the Lord is for ever, unchanging:
    While changing all things;
The word of the Lord is joy undeserved:
    Hope unexpected, love unstinting;
The word of the Lord is the beginning of the journey:
    And its end.

Which Passes All Understanding

The peace of God
Which passes all understanding
Is no still pool
Which, though perfectly reflective,
Reflects only
That peace within my understanding,
Only my own face.

Such human stillness
Is an absence, for here there is
No sound, no movement,
No breath of air. It proves an absence
Of being or feeling,
An absence of thought, relaxation
In the lack of questions.

God's peace passes,
Outruns and overturns our rest.
It is brimming
Full of presence, of living, moving,
Breathing, thinking,
Being. It is not still, but full,
Thrumming, piercing,

Purposeful,
Inevitable, disquieting,
A tinnitus,
The celestial harmony of the spheres,
If we could hear it,
The resonant frequency of the universe
Drawing in all things, all people.

Worcester Cathedral Triptych

I Cloister Garden

A clinking trowel and the rustle of a bird
Ricochets across, around the square.
Unseen voices and whispered footsteps, beyond
Clouded glass, circle the green stillness
Where imperceptible soughing of the air
Breathes above the green and living graves.

II Library

A charismatic silence folds viscous air
As soft, heavy pages crinkle,
And ink sparks with ancient light,
In my mortal eyes.

My briefly living hand brushes skin
Smoothed in another world by unknown
Hands. Words breathe and dance again
In my reading.

III Crypt

Beneath the thundering wash of marble and gilt,
And the flow of polished floor, is the simple, silent

Substrate – an undertow of low, white vaults.
Prayer flickers through the cavities and twines
Around the columnar roots as thought and feeling
Wax under the shadow of His wing.

JELLYFISH

Such an alien beauty glowing
With near-invisible translucence,
Swaying with the ebb and flow,
Seeming suspended in space and time.
Waiting.

An eternal insubstance
Incubated, nourished, encompassed
Only by, only in,
These amniotic waters, quite
Reliant.

Floating in a strange remission
Between vapour and solidity,
Between longing and completion,
Between hope and fulfilment is
My jellyfish soul.

Cherry Tree in Winter

This year, I saw my cherry tree transfigured,
Shiver with a bloom of spring insects,
A summer parliament of birds, concluding
With a flurry of chirruping wings at sunset,
The noisy thieving of crimson autumn fruit,
Before bright, silent leaves detach and drift
Softly, slowly, down, discarded one by one.

But its true epiphany is winter,
When branches rise, offering nascent buds
To pierce the ice, embracing winter light,
Bright tracery etched on snow-laden sky
Or anchored darkly into bronze sunrise,
And, on a numinous February night, burdened
With a universe of starry blossom.

Acknowledgements

I am indebted to Robyn Cadwallader whose fascinating novel *The Anchoress* inspired the poems in the titular sequence of poems entitled "Anchorage" and also had an influence on the poems on "Freedom" which follow it.

I should also like to acknowledge my debt to David Runcorn whose thoughtful Lent book, *Dust and Glory* initiated a number of poems in the collection, most notably the sequence on the Parable of the Prodigal Son and also "Saturday People" and "Which Passes All Understanding", and helped formulate the "Freedom" sequence.

And, as ever, thank you to my husband, Hanno, for your support in publishing this collection.

EZ

This book is printed on paper from sustainable sources managed under the Forest Stewardship Council (FSC) scheme.

It has been printed in the UK to reduce transportation miles and their impact upon the environment.

For every new title that Troubador publishes, we plant a tree to offset CO_2, partnering with the More Trees scheme.

For more about how Troubador offsets its environmental impact, see www.troubador.co.uk/sustainability-and-community